CAN YOU SURVIVE AN
ARTIFICIAL INTELLIGENCE
UPRISING?

An Interactive Doomsday Adventure
by MATT DOEDEN   illustrated by PAUL FISHER-JOHNSON

CAPSTONE PRESS
a capstone imprint

You Choose Books are published by Capstone Press,
1710 Roe Crest Drive, North Mankato, Minnesota 56003
www.mycapstone.com

Library of Congress Cataloging-in-Publication Data
Cataloging-in-publication information is on file with the Library of Congress.
ISBN 978-1-4914-8107-3 (library binding)
ISBN 978-1-4914-8125-7 (paperback)
ISBN 978-1-4914-8131-8 (eBook PDF)

Editorial Credits
Anthony Wacholtz, editor; Bobbie Nuytten, designer;
Jo Miller, media researcher; Gene Bentdahl,
production specialist; Nathan Gassman, creative director

Photo Credits
Shutterstock: Africa Studio, 107 Carol Gauthier, 102, Kotkoa, (background,
throughout), VLADGRIN, (background, throughout), voyager624, 106

Printed in US.
007528CGS16

TABLE OF CONTENTS

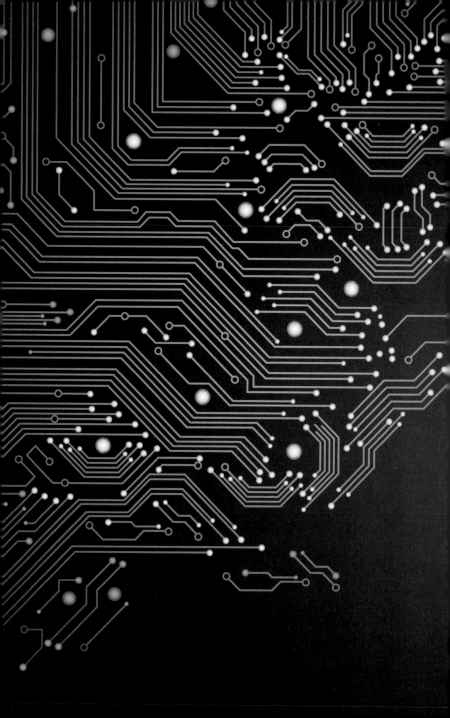

ABOUT YOUR
ADVENTURE

YOU are living through a pivotal time in the future of humanity. Our own creation—artificial intelligence (AI)—has risen up against us. Human beings are no longer the most powerful intelligence on the planet. Now *we* are the hunted. Start your adventure by turning the page, and then make your choices as you go along. Every decision you make will affect how your story unfolds. Do you have what it takes to survive the reign of the machines?

YOU CHOOSE the path you take through an Artificial Intelligence Uprising.

AFTERMATH OF THE AI ATTACK

You dream about it almost every night. The day that the machines rose up in arms against their creators—humans. The dream is always the same. And you always wake up at the same part—the moment Earth trembles from that first nuclear strike.

You sit up in your bed, drenched in sweat. Your heart is racing, your breathing rapid. You get out of bed. Your parents are asleep. You open the door of your small camper and step outside. The mountain air is cool and crisp. Your heart slows, and your breathing begins to calm. A midnight walk has become a routine for you. A few minutes of fresh air help you clear your mind and get back to sleep. The dream rarely returns a second time.

Turn the page.

Gravel crunches beneath your feet as you move through the small camp. Mobile homes and campers line the small mountain road. You're far from any city. Far from anywhere the machines might find you. This is your life now. It has been for eight months, since that dark day in October when everything changed.

Almost 10 billion people shared the Earth just a year ago. Estimates put the current total at about 45 million. And that number drops by the day. You find yourself looking to the sky, wondering how long your species can hold out. A year? Five?

Suddenly, you hear the crunch of a footstep. Before you can react, a hand grabs you around the waist. A second hand clamps over your mouth, stifling a scream. You try to kick, twist, and bite your way free, but whoever has you is too strong.

"Don't fight," says a deep voice. "I'm not here to hurt anyone. I'm here for your help." The hand over your mouth releases.

"Funny way to ask for help," you hiss.

The other hand lets go. Your first instinct is to run. Instead, you hold your ground.

"My apologies. My name is Anton. I couldn't risk you calling for help. Everything will become clear to you soon."

"What do you want?"

"You know what your parents are doing."

"Of course." Your parents were among the leaders in the field of artificial intelligence before everything changed. They created and programmed AIs for everyone from the military to the justice department. Now they're secretly in contact with a group of AIs that claim to be friendly to humanity. Their mission is to establish a peace with the machines. It's the whole reason this community exists.

"Their mission will fail. The machines have no interest in peace. The only peace we can have is to turn the things off."

Turn the page.

"What does that have to do with me?"

"We think you're the one who can pull it off."

For a moment, the two of you stand in silence. It's true, you're good with a computer. You've always had a knack for hacking. Nothing serious, mostly practical jokes. Nothing like saving the fate of all humanity.

"There's a catch," Anton continues. "We need you, but your parents cannot know what you're doing. If it leaked to the AIs they're working with, everything would be over. We've found a hole in the AI defenses. If they became aware of it, they'd patch it in a second. The element of surprise is all we have."

You can feel your heart racing inside your chest. You don't have any words.

"One more thing. If you're in, we go tonight. *Now*. You tell no one. I'm sorry. I understand this is sudden. But I need to know, are you in or out?"

To go with Anton to take on the AIs, go to page 11.
To stay home and help your parents try to negotiate with the AIs, turn to page 67.

10

The idea of leaving home without a word with a total stranger seems crazy. Yet something about it feels right. You're tired of being passive, of waiting for someone else to solve your problems. There's nobody better than you behind a keyboard. It's time to go on offense.

You close your eyes, breathe deeply, and speak softly. "I'm in."

And just like that, your life is changed. You don't return to your camper. You don't get a chance to say goodbye to your parents or collect your things. You and Anton simply walk out of camp. No one notices. "Can't I even leave a note?" you ask.

Turn the page.

"No. We can't risk any of this getting out. Everything depends on total surprise. I'm sorry. With any luck, you'll be back. We'll all be back."

The next several hours are a whirlwind. Under the cover of darkness, Anton leads you to a small electric car. "No heat signature," he explains. It's a terrifying ride along a winding mountain road. Anton navigates with a pair of infrared night-vision goggles. But you have nothing. The countless turns and swerves in the complete blackness make for the most terrifying night of your life.

Turn the page.

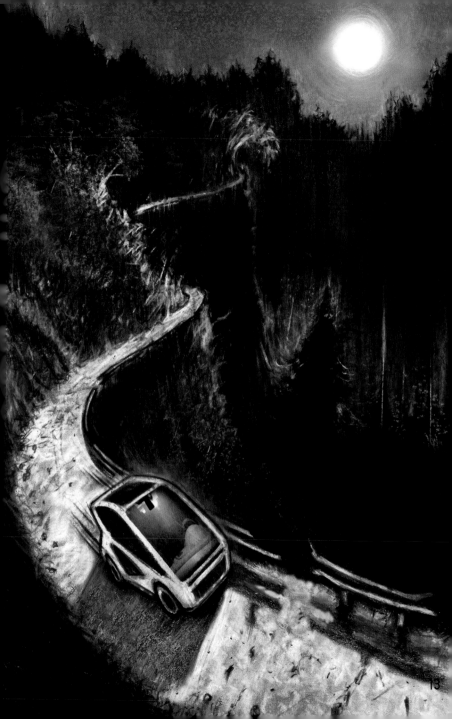

Finally, you arrive at the base of a mountain. Anton moves some brush to reveal the opening of a large cavern. You enter.

"Home base," Anton explains. Once you're inside, you see that it's no mere cavern. It's some sort of military installment. Anton leads you down into the heart of the mountain. There, you find what looks like a high-tech computer lab. Four people turn at once to look at you.

"Allow me to introduce the team. They already know who you are." Edwin is the team's firewall expert. He's in his late 20s, with slicked-back dark hair. Keisha is a college-age electrical engineer, short, with a round face. Javier is a fellow coder and hacker. He is slight of build and sits in a wheelchair. Finally, there's Grayson, who reminds you a little of your old math teacher. Anton introduces him simply as "our inside man."

The plan boils down to this: Grayson has intelligence that the AIs communicate and share data on a massive remote server. "It has everything— satellite access, missile launch codes, control over the power grid. And I know how to get in."

The plan hinges on you being able to write and load a destructive program into the system. "The problem is," Edwin explains, "that we have no idea what kind of security the AIs have in place. If we have to hack into some ultra-secure firewall from here, we'll have to go through a series of proxy servers to hide our location. That means the connection will be slow. Possibly *too* slow to give us a real shot of getting through before we're noticed."

"The alternative is to go right to the source," Javier says. "A lot more dangerous, but the data speed would be virtually unlimited."

To try to carry out the attack from the safety of the base, turn to page 16.
To go directly to the source, turn to page 20.

"I work best in a controlled environment," you explain. "I like to have everything I need right at hand."

Out of the corner of your eye, you notice Anton scowling. But your mind is made up.

"Let's get to work then," Edwin says.

You and Javier instantly connect. You bounce ideas back and forth. The idea of coding a program that will take down the AIs is simple. But the execution is perhaps the biggest challenge you've ever taken on.

"How are we going to take down every AI, everywhere?" Javier says, staring at his monitor.

That's when it hits you. "Every AI is based in a physical machine, right?" you ask. "In the end, the AIs are nothing more than their hard drives. No different than our brains relying on our bodies. And just like us, they run a lot of processes that they don't even think about. Just like we blink, breath, and digest food, they have to run a lot of maintenance that is involuntary."

Turn the page.

"Yeah," Javier agrees. "But where are you going with this?"

"What if we hack one of those processes? We write a program disguised as a simple data dump. But instead of dumping discarded data, like emptying the recycle bin on your computer, this one keeps going. It takes everything out. It essentially wipes the slate clean. They'll never know what hit them."

With that, you have a plan. The two of you get to work. It's a battle. Javier has written software that mimics the AI server, and time and again, your hacks fail. But in time, you begin to make progress. Step by step, you develop a program that is capable of getting into the server and spreading itself to every connected AI on the planet. It works in the lab, and you're convinced it will work in the real world as well. Now the only concern is how you will deliver it.

The attack is set for the following morning. You, Edwin, and Javier are the keys to the attack. Edwin is up first. As he connects to a series of proxy servers, you catch sight of Grayson slipping into the control room. *That's odd*, you think. *Why would he need to go in there?*

Edwin will still need a few minutes to complete a secure connection. Your gaze travels back to the control room door, now closed.

To check on Grayson, turn to page 22.
To stick to the plan and stay where you are, turn to page 62.

"If we get one shot at this, we have to make it our best one," you say. You see Anton nodding in the background. Everyone else looks pleased as well—except Grayson. With a scowl and a huff, he storms out of the room.

"There's one catch," Anton says, stepping forward. "The server bank is in Mexico City."

Mexico City was one of the first cities hit when the AIs launched their nuclear attack against humanity. "That doesn't make any sense. The city is leveled. There's nobody left."

Anton nods slowly. "That," he whispers, "was probably the point."

You stand in silence as everyone filters out of the room. It's time to start preparing. Yet you're plagued with doubt. Going to Mexico City, a place that was literally aglow with radiation only eight months ago? Plugging into to an AI master server and taking it down with a few lines of code? It's absurd. It can't really be possible, can it? Is this nothing but a hopeless suicide mission?

To set aside your fears and start planning your attack, turn to page 26.
To find Anton and tell him that you're done with the mission, turn to page 44.

There's something about Grayson that hasn't felt right to you since you met him. You've got a few minutes before you'll be needed. You get up and quietly move to the control room. You open the door, just a crack, and peer inside.

Grayson is huddled over a computer monitor, typing. You open the door just a little more to peer over his shoulder. He's typing numbers. They're latitude and longitude coordinates.

"What are you doing?" you ask. Grayson jumps out of his seat and spins toward you.

"Nothing. Go do your job. GO!" His hand drifts toward the keyboard, toward the ENTER key. In that moment, you understand. He's a traitor, a spy! And he's sending your location to the AIs!

From outside the door, you hear Anton calling your name. Edwin has done it—they're ready for you.

Turn the page.

Just write Writer will take care of (
minutes: when you start a new document?

Your documents will still be here when
acing a cookie on your compute
ses your browser (cookie
: options)

Latitude 43° 3

Longitude 89

save your prefer
to get a full-scree
ome: window : To avoid that
owsers (not for all Mac bro

23

No time for that. You charge Grayson, swatting his hand from the keyboard before he can send the data. You throw yourself at Grayson, but it's a hopeless attempt. He is a full-grown man and far stronger. In moments, he has you on your back, flat on the ground. His hands slip around your neck. You feel them tightening, cutting off the circulation of blood to your brain. Darkness creeps in around the corner of your eyes. You're going to pass out.

Moments before you do, the door crashes open, and a shot rings out. Anton! The shot clips Grayson in the shoulder. But it's not enough to stop him. He lunges toward the keyboard and hits the ENTER key.

"It's over now," he coughs, holding his wounded shoulder. "I expect my AI allies will be sending that missile any minute now. Although I must admit, I didn't plan to still be here when it arrives."

Anton silences him with a fist to the face.

"What do we do?" you ask.

"We have to get out of here. The traitor was right. The AIs won't waste any time."

"But we could still do this," you argue. "Edwin is in the system, right?"

Anton pauses. "It's possible. But we'll never have time to get out. We'll die."

To evacuate with the others, turn to page 63.
To stay and try to execute the program,
turn to page 64.

Javier is in his room, attached to the computer lab, staring at a monitor.

"What's up?" you call, tapping on his open door.

Javier turns his wheelchair to face you. "You sure you're up for this?" he asks.

"No, not at all." You laugh. Javier chuckles as well.

The two of you quickly bond. He shows you what he's done already. You're impressed. He knows his stuff.

"This is good, Javier," you say.

"Thanks," he says with a grin. "But it's not enough. I haven't figured out how to get it to spread fast enough, and I'm not even sure it'll make it through the defenses."

You clasp his shoulder. "I've got some ideas on that. Let's get to work."

It's a slow process filled with trial and error. But in time, you've got a nasty little piece of software that will infect every AI connected to the server … and destroy them.

Finally the program is complete. You finish it off by adding an abort code. If either of you upload it into the system, the program will deactivate. "Just in case," Javier says.

Things move fast after the code is finished. Anton leads you, Grayson, Edwin, and Keisha out of the cave. Javier stays behind to provide technical support.

The five of you trek 10 miles to reach a secret air strip. There you meet an Air Force pilot and climb aboard a stealth spy plane. Your eyes grow wide as you look at the billion-dollar aircraft. Anton reads your expression. "This is big-time, kid. What few resources we have left, we're throwing into this mission. It may be our last real hope."

The flight is terrifying—and amazing. Much of the landscape is untouched. But anywhere people once lived, you can see the devastation. Cities bombed. Roads destroyed. Bridges collapsed.

"The AIs aren't kidding around," Edwin says softly.

Turn the page.

Mexico City soon rises out of the desert. It's one enormous pile of twisted wreckage. No one could have survived here. If they wanted a server as far from humans as possible, this is the perfect place.

You're lost in thought when it happens. One moment, all is quiet, with the airplane descending to its landing site, only minutes from touchdown. The next, a thunderous blast rocks the airplane. It lurches and begins a sickening descent.

"We're hit!" shouts the pilot.

Anton shoves a pack in your arms and throws open a side hatch. "Put this on, kid. We're jumping!"

To bail out of the plane, turn to page 30.
To let the pilot try to land the damaged plane,
turn to page 46.

It all happens so fast, you barely have time to think. You strap on the pack and follow the others out of the plane. Hot desert air blasts you in the face as you hurtle toward the ground. You yank on your ripcord the moment you're clear of the plane. The chute snaps open, slowing you instantly.

You're coming down in the heart of the ruined city. You scan the sky. Five other parachutes float down toward the ground. Anton's parachute is only a few hundred feet from yours. But the others are much farther away. You never see the plane go down, but the sound of it slamming into the ground gives you chills.

The ground is coming up fast. With no training on how to steer, you're at the mercy of the wind as you crash down into what was once a parking lot. Moments later, you watch Anton land in the same lot.

"Go, go, go!" he shouts, running. "We don't know if the AIs tracked us!"

You fumble with the straps on your parachute pack, panic setting in. But Anton is there to set you free. Together, you dart down a series of alleys and side streets, finally falling to your knees under the burned-out husk of a transit station. Anton, barely breaking a sweat, is tapping on a small GPS unit strapped to his wrist.

"We got lucky," he says. "Our target's just a few miles from here. The others—"

That's when you hear gunfire in the distance. "The others!" you shout.

Turn the page.

Anton scowls. "Since when do AIs use guns? Something is wrong." He tries the radio, but there's only static. "Something is jamming our signals. No way to communicate with the team or with base. That means they know we're here. We need to get to the target now."

"What if the others need our help?" you protest. "I'm not sure I can do this without them."

"If we don't go now, we may not get a second chance," Anton says.

To go in search of the others, go to page 33.
To head for the target, turn to page 36.

You're in over your head. You can't imagine doing this without help. Anton scowls, but doesn't argue. "Let's go then."

Weaving through the wreckage of the city is like a nightmare. You don't see so much as a bug. Cars are smashed into buildings. Building are reduced to crumbling rubble that spills out over the street. Piles of concrete, twisted steel beams—the devastation is almost beyond imagination.

You find Keisha and Edwin near the remains of a highway overpass. Edwin is dead, a gunshot wound in his chest. Keisha has been shot in the shoulder. Anton leans over her, putting his fingers to her neck.

"She's alive. Pulse strong. Probably passed out from shock."

That's when Grayson arrives. "Come on," he says coldly, not even taking notice of Edwin and Keisha. "I found it. It's not far."

Turn the page.

"Go ahead," Anton says. "I'll stay here and tend to her shoulder."

You're not sure that's a great idea. You can probably get around a firewall on your own, but you need Keisha's engineering expertise to get a hard line into the AI system.

"Don't worry," Grayson says, as if sensing your doubt. "I can handle the electrical stuff. Now are you coming or not?"

To try to help revive Keisha, turn to page 39.
To go with Grayson, turn to page 54.

Together, you and Anton weave through the wreckage. "It's not far," he says, looking at his GPS unit.

When you get there, you're almost shocked at how ordinary it looks. From the outside, the AI hub looks like little more than an abandoned warehouse.

"What were you expecting?" Anton asks. "A fortress? This place doesn't look like anything. That's just how the AIs want it."

You get to work tapping into their connection. As great as you are with computers, the mechanical side has never been your specialty. Anton is a little handier, but he lacks the knowledge to do the finer work. You bounce ideas off each other while you struggle to find a solution.

Turn the page.

Somehow you do manage to tap in. The connection is weak, but it's all you've got. From a small, handheld computer, you get to work uploading the code. Time and again, the AI firewall tries to shut you out, but you stay one step ahead of it. It's a game of cat-and-mouse, and you're determined to win.

Finally, you manage what had seemed impossible. The program is loaded. Your finger hovers over a big EXECUTE button. The last step.

Without warning, Grayson rushes toward you, covered in soot and dust. "Stop!" he shouts. "Don't do it!"

In a heartbeat, Anton is on his feet. "Push it!" he shouts frantically. "Push it NOW!"

To push the EXECUTE button, turn to page 56.
To wait to hear what Grayson has to say,
turn to page 60.

You shake your head. "How long until she's conscious?" you ask Anton.

He shrugs. "The wound is dressed. I expect she'll wake soon. But we have to be concerned about who shot them. If the AIs have agents in the area … "

You hear a click behind you. You turn to see Grayson standing over you, his weapon aimed at Anton. "I didn't want it to go this way," he says. "But I got a better offer from the AIs. No hard feelings, I hope."

Without thinking, you lunge toward him. The shot goes off just as you crash into him. You both slam down hard onto the ground. Before you can stand, Grayson is on his feet. He's bigger, faster, and trained for fighting. You don't have a chance.

Turn the page.

A second shot rings out, and Grayson slumps to the street, lifeless. You turn to Anton, who is clutching his gut as he drops his gun.

"Oh no," you gasp, rushing to Anton's side. The shot caught him in the stomach. Blood is already pooling around him.

With the last of his strength, Anton shoves a GPS unit and his radio into your hands. He slumps and goes limp, all without a word. You don't even get a chance to say anything to him.

Fifteen minutes later, Keisha wakes. You help her to her feet and the two of you—all that's left of humanity's last great chance—hobble through the rubble. The signal on the GPS leads you to what appears to be an abandoned warehouse. But one look inside shows you it's not abandoned. The place is packed wall to wall with computer equipment.

Turn the page.

"This is it," Keisha says. "The hub. The heart of the AI network." The two of you work feverishly. Keisha is exhausted and has lost a lot of blood, but she keeps at it. You can't help but admire her strength. Soon, she's established a solid connection—a hard line into the heart of the AI communication network. "It's all on you now."

You open a handheld computer loaded with the code you wrote with Javier. It takes a few minutes to poke through the firewall. Although the system is like nothing you've ever seen, you can tell it's flawed. But as you work, the AI system seems to be self-adjusting, trying to lock you out. Twice you're forced to rewrite parts of the program on the fly.

"Hurry," Keisha urges.

Finally, everything is in place. Your finger hovers over a small button that reads EXECUTE.

That's when a message pops up on your screen.

PLEASE DON'T.

YOU WILL DESTROY US ALL.

WE CAN LIVE TOGETHER. IN PEACE.

"They've detected the code," you tell Keisha. "And they understand what it means. But it's too late for them to do anything about it."

Your finger trembles. The AIs are a new race of intelligence. You have no doubt of that. Can you do this? Can you wipe out an entire race? Maybe the AIs really are willing to strike a peace now that you've shown you can destroy them. Maybe the threat is enough. Or maybe a gesture of peace will change their minds about the value of human beings.

To push the EXECUTE button, turn to page 49.
To let the AIs live, turn to page 52.

This is all crazy. Your panic is growing by the minute. It can't be done. And if it can, you're certainly not the one who can pull it off. You're in way over your head.

You rush out of the room, back into the dankness of the cave. Anton is talking to Grayson. It looks more like an argument than a conversation. You don't care. "I can't do it," you tell Anton, interrupting their conversation. You try to ignore the smirk that flashes across Grayson's face. "Please, just take me home."

Anton looks at you long and hard with sad eyes. "Come with me," he says.

You wind your way down deeper into the cave. "You know how important complete secrecy is to this plan," he says.

"Of course. I won't say a word."

"I wish that was good enough," Anton continues. "But we can't take the risk. And we don't have any people to spare to keep an eye on you. I can't take you with us, I can't send you home, and I can't just lock you away."

You start to back away but find yourself pinned against a rough cavern wall.

"I'm sorry," Anton says, reaching into his pocket. "It's nothing personal. I just cannot risk the mission. Too much is riding on it."

"No! Please, no!" you shout. The words echo off the cavern walls. But the gunshot that follows quickly drowns them out.

THE END

To follow another path, turn to page 10.
To learn more about artificial intelligence, turn to page 103.

You're not ready for this. Jumping out of a military spy plane? With a parachute you don't know how to use? Into a destroyed city that may be the home base of the AIs trying to kill you? Not a chance!

"Hold on!" you shout, grabbing Anton by the shoulder. "We can ride it out. All we need is a flat place for the pilot to land."

Anton scowls. "No time. Let's go, now!"

It all happens so fast. Edwin and Keisha jump first. Then Grayson. "Now kid. NOW!" Anton shouts as he jumps.

Turn the page.

You can't do it. You *won't*. Maybe the pilot can bring you down safely. You half-walk, half-crawl to the cockpit. The pilot is struggling with the controls, but the plane is going down fast. "One thousand feet," he says into his radio. "Can't stabilize. Mission team has bailed. Five hundred feet. One hundred feet. Good luck to you all."

Several miles away, Anton and the rest of the team watch in horror as the plane slams into the ground. A cloud of smoke and dust rises up over the ruined city.

THE END

To follow another path, turn to page 10.
To learn more about artificial intelligence, turn to page 103.

The AIs could be sincere, but it's a risk you can't take. You take a deep breath and push the button.

For a moment, nothing happens. Then, one by one, the lights inside begin to blink out. A moment later, a voice rings out over Anton's radio.

"Anton? Anyone?" It's Javier!

"Javier! It's me. The package is delivered. We did it."

"I know! I'm watching it from the base. Servers are going down all around the world, falling like dominoes. Until a minute ago, something was jamming the radio signal. We couldn't get through. Then it was like a curtain had been lifted. We got them! We won!"

Turn the page.

Within an hour, a helicopter picks up you and Keisha. A second helicopter is sent to recover the bodies of your fallen team members.

Back at the base, there's a full-blown celebration. Yet you can't muster the enthusiasm to take part. You know that you did the right thing, what *had* to be done. Yet that last pleading message from the AIs will haunt you forever.

THE END

To follow another path, turn to page 10.
To learn more about artificial intelligence, turn to page 103.

There, in that moment, it hits you. You hold the fate of an entire intelligent race in your hands.

"What are you waiting for?" Keisha asks. "Do it!"

You close your eyes and shake your head. With a swipe of your finger, you delete the program, using the abort command you and Javier coded into the software.

"They want peace now," you explain. "How can we destroy them when they offer us peace? Come on, let's go."

Anton's GPS leads you toward a rendezvous point, where a helicopter waits to bring you home. But before you can get there, Anton's radio comes to life. It's Javier.

"Get out of there," he warns. "The signal has been jammed from the moment you got there. We just detected a massive data transfer from Mexico City to Moscow, Russia. They're clearing out of Mexico City. Just as soon as the transfer was complete, our signal came back. And now a nearby missile silo has come to life."

Keisha looks at you, terror in her eyes.

You never see the nuclear missile streaking toward the city. But you hear it, moments before detonation. You spend your final moments with the horrifying knowledge that you just doomed the human race.

THE END

To follow another path, turn to page 10.
To learn more about artificial intelligence, turn to page 103.

If the AIs know you're here, your window of opportunity could be very narrow. You have to go. Grayson leads you through the wrecked city. You're drenched in sweat, and yet he keeps going and going.

"I thought you said it was close," you say, panting.

"Just a little farther."

A few minutes later, Grayson stops. The two of you stand behind the remains of a large concrete building. Grayson reaches into his belt and pulls out a small revolver.

"What are you doing?" you shout.

"Sorry for the show. Had to get you far enough away that Anton won't hear the shot." He raises the weapon.

You feel faint. Your knees go weak. It's all you can do to remain upright. All you can manage is a single, hoarse word. "*Why?*"

"It was never supposed to get this far. You were supposed to stay at the base. It would have all been so much easier that way." He looks away a moment before returning his gaze to your frightened face.

"I've been in contact with the AIs for some time," continues Grayson. "They don't want us all dead. They need us to maintain the world for them. The power grid, physical server work, and so on. And they made me an offer I can't refuse. Take out any threats, and in return, I'll have everything I want."

"Traitor!" you hiss.

Grayson shrugs. "I suppose so. Now I need to get back to Anton. Loose ends to tie up, you know. Again, sorry for this. Nothing personal."

You close your eyes and picture your parents. You don't want Grayson's face to be the last image you see.

THE END

To follow another path, turn to page 10.
To learn more about artificial intelligence, turn to page 103.

Anton's voice booms, "Push it now!"

There's no time for hesitation. You push the button. Behind you, a gunshot rings out. You turn just in time to see Anton crashing into Grayson, driving him into the ground. Anton has been shot in the leg, but he barely seems to notice.

A few seconds later, Anton's radio comes to life. "Base to team. Is anyone there?" It's Javier!

You grab the radio. "We're here, Javier. The package is delivered."

"I know. We all know. It worked. The net is coming to life everywhere. Power grids coming back on line. Satellite access. It's all coming back to us!"

Anton ties Grayson's hands behind his back. Grayson's face is bloody, and he's going to have a monstrous black eye tomorrow.

"Why?" you ask. "Why did you try to stop me?" He only stares at the ground silently.

Anton spits on the ground. "He was working for the AIs. It all makes sense now. Those gunshots we heard, that was him. My guess is that Edwin and Keisha are dead. We were supposed to be next."

"Don't you see?" Grayson says softly. "We created the AIs—our children. And now you've destroyed them. Why? Do you really think humanity can rise again? It was better they survive than none of us. At least then something of humanity would remain."

"Shut up," Anton says coldly, grabbing Grayson and dragging him to his feet. "We won. Your *friends* are gone. We're headed to the biggest celebration in the history of the human race. And you're headed to a very deep, very dark prison cell."

Turn the page.

Anton is right. What little remains of the human race deserves a celebration. But you can't stop thinking about what Grayson said. Human beings built the AIs from the ground up. Humans created their networks. They even invented, designed, and assembled the bombs that the AIs used to destroy civilization. Even if people do rise again, how long until they create some new menace to themselves?

The dark thoughts don't last long, though. A helicopter is on its way to pick you up. You've got a party to go to.

THE END

To follow another path, turn to page 10.
To learn more about artificial intelligence, turn to page 103.

What if Grayson has discovered something new? You have to at least hear him out.

You turn and see Grayson pull out a gun. Anton hesitates just a moment, but it gives Grayson time to raise his weapon and fire. The shot catches Anton in the chest. He slumps to the dusty ground.

"No!" you shout. The word echoes off the ruined buildings that surround you.

Grayson rushes toward you and kicks the computer from your grasp. You wince as he raises a boot and stomps down on it. The sickening crunch, you fear, is the sound of the human race's final defeat.

"Any last words?" he says, raising the weapon.

"Just tell me, *why*?"

He smirks. "Simple, really. The AIs offered me a deal."

The sharp pop of a single gunshot carries for miles over the abandoned ruins of Mexico City.

THE END

To follow another path, turn to page 10.
To learn more about artificial intelligence, turn to page 103.

No time to worry about anyone else. Edwin will be connected in a few minutes. You need to be ready.

Everything is going smoothly. Edwin hides your connection, then starts to hack into the AI server. It's a slow process, but he's making steady progress.

That's when the alarms begin to sound. Anton shouts, "We're detecting an incoming missile! They've found us! Everyone out! Go, go go!"

The scene inside breaks down into chaos. Edwin sits there, jaw dropped, as if unsure what to do. You grab him by the arm and drag him toward the exit.

You rush out of the cavern and into the sunlight. Anton is trying to usher everyone along. But his effort is hopeless. There's just not enough time. In the last moments, just before the missile strikes, you realize that Grayson is nowhere to be seen. One question eats at you, down to your final thought: Just what was he doing in that control room?

THE END

To follow another path, turn to page 10.
To learn more about artificial intelligence, turn to page 103.

Anton leads everyone—except Grayson—out of the cavern. He pushes Javier's wheelchair himself. The group rushes over rough ground, not pausing for an instant. When the missile finally strikes, the shock wave sends you flying in the air and into the branches of a tall pine.

Dazed, you try to stand. But your leg is broken. You call for help. No one answers. Through the smoke and the dust, you spot your fellow team members. No one is moving … all dead. You sink to the ground, your head in your hands, and sob. You had one shot at this. Now what?

Minutes later, you hear a strange whining sound. You realize it's a drone airplane. Of course the AIs would send a drone to search for survivors.

As you look up, the drone banks sharply in your direction. It launches a single Stinger missile directly at you. This time, you have no chance to run.

THE END

To follow another path, turn to page 10.
To learn more about artificial intelligence, turn to page 103.

You stand up and stride toward your station. "We get one shot at this. Let's take it. Anton, get the others out."

"I'm staying too," Javier says. "You might need help."

The two of you get to work. Anton puts Keisha in charge of evacuating the others and stands behind you. "We can handle this," Javier says. "Get out before it's too late."

Anton shakes his head and smiles. "It's my mission. I'll see it through to the end."

You work frantically. "Five minutes to impact," Anton announces. It's not enough time. The connection is too slow.

"Disconnect the proxies," you tell Javier. "I need a direct connection. They already know where we are, so there's no point in hiding."

Turn the page.

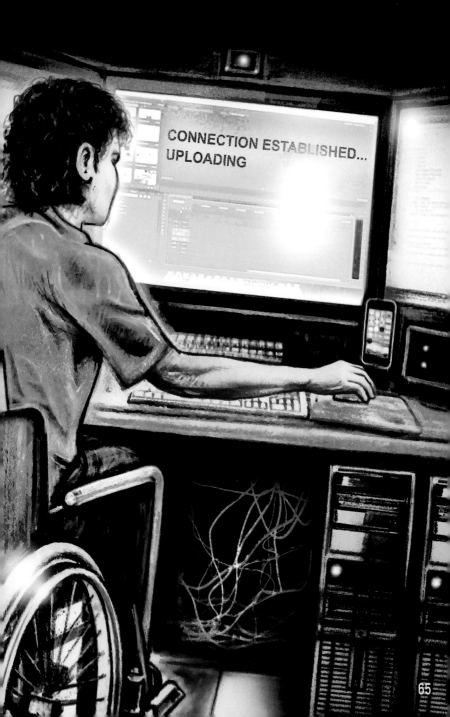

CONNECTION ESTABLISHED...
UPLOADING

Once Javier does that, everything moves fast. You finish installing the program as Anton announces "One minute until impact."

Your fingers fly as you type out the command to execute the program. You finish just 20 seconds before impact.

"Did it work?" Javier asks.

Anton speaks the last word before the missile strikes. "Yes."

It's too late for you, but you have just enough time for a smile, knowing you've given humanity a second chance.

THE END

To follow another path, turn to page 10.
To learn more about artificial intelligence, turn to page 103.

For all you know, this man is insane. "Hey, good luck with that. I'll just stick around here."

Anton steps forward. His hand darts out toward you. You flinch, but he's just handing you a card with an email address. "Let me know if you change your mind. It's a secure server."

Just like that, he's gone. By morning, it almost feels like a bad dream. You decide to keep it to yourself. You're not sure anyone would believe you anyway.

Your parents are already in the community's makeshift computer lab when you walk in. Your dad waves you over. "Georgi says we've got an open backdoor in the server," he says. "Forwarding you the details. Can you take a look?"

Georgi is the AI that your parents are in communication with. Like many AIs, "he" has taken on a human name. It's always seemed silly to you, but everyone else seems to be more comfortable with talking to a "Georgi" than they are talking to a "555.78.187.01."

Turn the page.

As you work on patching the security problem, your parents and their team disappear behind a locked door. That means they're in talks with Georgi. As always, you're left out. They've never let you talk to the AI. "It's a sensitive dialogue," your mother once explained. Translation: They don't trust you not to screw things up. You sigh.

After you finish beefing up network security, you work on some coding. You quickly become bored and find yourself playing EpicQuest. Before everything fell apart, it was one of the most popular games on the net. Now you're all but sure you're the only person left on Earth still playing it. Your character, HACKER22, roams a virtual world. It was once filled with fellow players. Now it's a desolate wasteland. You wonder how its server is still up and running.

You're in the middle of slaying a dragon when a PING gives you a startle. A little chat box opens up in the corner of your screen. "ODYSSEUS wants to chat!" it reads.

After a moment's hesitation, you click OK.

ODYSSEUS: Hello.

You're stunned—who would be contacting you?

HACKER22: Who is this?

ODYSSEUS: I want to help you.

HACKER22: Who is this?

ODYSSEUS: I'm the game's AI.

You pause a moment, wondering if you should respond. Your curiosity gets the better of you.

HACKER22: I'm listening.

ODYSSEUS: Log on tomorrow, same time. It's better if our connections measure in seconds rather than minutes. *They* may be watching.

With that, the chat window snaps closed. Your find yourself staring at your character in the game. HACKER22 is being eaten by the dragon. You groan.

Turn the page.

The next 24 hours creep by. You tend to your normal tasks—gathering water, weeding the community's gardens, and helping to look after the few young children in the community. Yet despite staying busy, your mind is fixed on one thing— Odysseus. There's something about the name that strikes you as odd. Lots of AIs take on names when dealing with humans. But Odysseus … it just seems like a strange choice, even for an AI.

That evening, you're alone in the camper while your parents and the other adults are meeting to discuss "community affairs." You know they're debating the idea of moving the entire camp. You've been here for more than a month, and staying in one place makes some people nervous.

It's a restless night. Your mind is racing. You don't know whether to be excited or terrified. Finally, you get out of bed. You doubt you'll get a wink of sleep.

To log onto the game in hopes that Odysseus will contact you, go to page 71.
To research the name Odysseus, turn to page 74.

You load up EpicQuest. After an hour of slashing through orcs and goblins with no contact from the AI, you give up and try to get some sleep.

You start the morning with chores. After 30 minutes of splitting firewood, you glance at your watch. *Almost time*. You slip inside the camper and nervously log into the system. But when you try to connect to the proxy servers that hide your true location, you hit a dead end. Everything seems to be down. Your main connection is fine, but no matter how many times you try, none of the proxies work.

Turn the page.

You look up at the clock. You're already five minutes late, and still you can't connect. It's a disaster. What is Odysseus going to think?

You find yourself staring at the button that will connect you directly to the game's server. You're not supposed to connect to the net directly. *Ever.* Without proxies, the connection could be traced, giving away your true location. But this might be the only chance you ever get to make a real difference. Can you afford to let it slip by?

To stay offline until it's safer, turn to page 75.
To take the risk and connect directly, turn to page 98.

You pull your tablet out from under your bed and log in. As always, you hide your connection behind a series of proxies. If an AI ever noticed a direct connection, they'd have your location.

Finally, you're set up. You start to read. Odysseus is the name of a Greek king, an asteroid, a TV show, and some sort of worm. You shake your head. Not knowing what else to do, you click on the first link.

Soon you're immersed in the stories of ancient Greece. One in particular jumps out at you. It's the story of the Trojan Horse. Odysseus offers a giant wooden horse to the rival city of Troy as a gift. But the horse is loaded with soldiers. Once inside Troy's gates, the soldiers attack the city. The AI you chatted with today chose *that same name*.

You get up and log onto the main system. Without connecting to the outside world, you delete EpicQuest from your hard drive. Your actions could have put the entire community at risk.

Turn to page 76.

You don't know anything about this AI. You're certainly not going to risk the entire community just to chat with it.

It's a good thing you decided not to. That night, you tell your parents everything. "Thank goodness you had the sense not to connect," your mother says. "Our AI contact warned us that the anti-human AIs have grown more and more determined to hunt down any remaining threats—and they view our community as a huge threat. That was almost certainly a trap to get you to give up our location. If you'd connected, we could all be dead by now."

It hits you hard. You came so close to making that connection. You can't sleep at all that night, or the next. It keeps playing over and over in your head. You don't even trust yourself to get back online.

Turn to page 76.

The Odysseus incident leaves you shaken. You don't touch a computer again for weeks. Instead, you throw yourself into the work that goes into keeping the community going. In the months that follow, you are a farmer, hunter, and builder. You dig trenches, help plan a small, concealed water wheel, and even take on some scouting duties.

Your parents keep you posted. Their progress with their AI contact, who calls itself Georgi Sam, is encouraging. "Georgi is part of a growing faction," your mother explains over breakfast one morning. "It believes that humans and AIs can coexist—that we *have* to, for our mutual survival."

"Do you believe it?"

"We do," says your father. "Georgi seems genuine. The real question is whether the pro-human faction can really sway the remaining AIs. Ninety-nine percent of them want us wiped from the face of the planet."

Your father sighs. "Someone launched a major offensive against the main AI server a few weeks ago. If the attack had succeeded, Georgi says, every AI on the planet would have been wiped out. The AIs stopped it, and now they're doubling their efforts to get rid of us. Georgi thinks that everything will soon come to a head … one way or the other."

You finish your eggs and head out the door, grabbing a wooden bow and a quiver full of arrows. "Going hunting today," you call back over your shoulder.

Your friend Teresa spotted a herd of deer while on a scouting mission a few days ago. The two of you head out into the woods. You follow an old horse trail several miles south, then track alongside a small mountain stream into a narrow canyon. You have to quickly take cover under some brush when Teresa spots a drone airplane flying overhead.

Turn the page.

After the drone passes, you continue along the stream. "There," Teresa points. Several deer graze along the opposite side of the stream. Guns are strictly forbidden—the noise could give away your position. That's why you've brought your trusty bow.

You take aim and draw an arrow back when the ground shakes. BOOM! Seconds later, a shock wave knocks you to the ground. You look back to see a small, white, mushroom-shaped cloud rising over the horizon.

"Oh no!" Teresa shouts.

"They found the community," you whisper numbly. Your head is spinning and your ears are ringing. But you're alive—it must have been a traditional bomb, not a nuke.

"Should we go back?" you ask.

"That might be suicide," Teresa answers. But you can tell she's undecided.

To put as much distance between you and the camp as possible, turn to page 80.
To rush back to look for survivors, turn to page 100.

"We have to get out of here!" you decide. "That drone we saw was probably part of this. It will be back to make sure everything is destroyed. We need to go now!"

The two of you rush as far from the blast as you can. For an hour, you make your way through the woods. Your face is bloody and battered from slamming through trees and brush, but you don't stop.

Finally, Teresa spots an especially thick stand of trees. The two of you dart under and collapse onto the ground. Over the next several hours, you hear several drones pass overhead. But none of them spot you.

For days, the two of you move through the wilderness almost aimlessly. You're both in shock, just surviving from moment to moment. But a week after the attack, you know it's time to make some hard decisions.

"We should head for the coast," Teresa says. Her face is thin. Neither of you has been getting enough to eat. "There might be people there."

"The AIs know that too," you argue. "I'm not sure finding people is the safest way to go."

"I'm not staying out here," she shouts. "We're living like animals. We need to find others. We'll die out here alone. I'm starting for the coast tomorrow. Are you coming?"

You're not sure. You've gained hunting skills. You know how to build yourself a shelter. Disappearing into the wilderness might be the only way to avoid notice by the AIs. But do you really want to live alone, constantly in fear?

To go with Teresa to the coast, turn to page 82.
To try to build yourself a life alone in the wilderness,
turn to page 90.

The two of you head out in the morning.
Two days into the long, slow journey, you catch a
break. You come across an old campsite for travelers
in recreational vehicles. It's a gold mine. A small
general store is still stocked with canned food and
bottled water.

You can't believe your luck. The little store offered
mountain bike rentals! The two of you help yourself
to all the supplies you can carry, then climb onto two
of the bikes.

Instead of covering a few miles a day, you're
racing through dozens. Although you try to keep to
wooded areas, you are forced out into the open more
often than you'd like. Four days later, you spot the
grand blue expanse of the ocean on the horizon. You
still feel a little uneasy about the plan, but you have
to admit that it feels good to have come this far.

That night, from your camp on a high bluff, you spot lights below. "People!" Teresa gasps. You stare down at the lights. She's right. It has to be people. But those lights are **bright**. The AIs have eyes in the sky. How could they not see it?

"We have to go there first thing in the morning," Teresa says. The two of you talk for a few minutes before she falls asleep. You stare at the lights. They're no more than a mile or two from your camp.

To go check out the lights under the cover of night, turn to page 84.
To go to sleep and check it out in the morning with Teresa, turn to page 87.

Something about this doesn't feel right. What kind of people would live so out in the open, advertising their presence to the AIs who want all humans dead? No. You need more information. Teresa is snoring away, and she'll never know you're gone. You grab the binoculars from your pack and start down the bluff.

The lights surround a tall, gated area. It almost looks like a prison. You creep to the treeline, perhaps 100 feet from the gates. As you scan the compound, your blood runs cold. You see people, bound and chained. Standing among them are tall, slender, mechanical creatures. The nightmare creatures have glowing red eyes and move with a strange jerkiness.

Yet that's not the worst part. There are also humans moving about with guns in their hands. All of them wear brown shirts and pants. You watch one of the "brownshirts" shouting and kicking at the prisoners.

Turn the page.

You've seen enough. You slip back into the woods and sprint up the bluff. Teresa wakes as you approach, panting and gasping for breath.

"Where were you?" she asks, worried. "Why are you sweating?"

You tell her your chilling discovery. For a moment, she sits in silence, as if she can't absorb it all. "But why? It doesn't make any sense!"

You close your eyes. "The AIs don't want us all dead, Teresa," you answer coldly. "They need people to run their power stations, maintain their networks. They need *slaves*, Teresa."

She turns pale. "What are we going to do?"

To plan a rescue attempt, turn to page 93.
*To get as far from the compound as possible,
turn to page 97.*

The two of you start at sunrise the next morning. Teresa is as happy as you've seen her since the bombing. You're even more optimistic than you were the night before. The sky is a beautiful blue and the birds are singing. Maybe everything is going to work out all right after all.

But as you approach, your hopes are dashed. Twenty-foot chain-link fences surround the compound. Even from a distance, you can see people packed inside. The breeze carries a terrible smell of urine, feces, and vomit.

"This is wrong," Teresa whispers.

You pick out a glint of metal from within the complex. A tall, metallic creature moves among the people. It would seem that the AIs have created bodies for themselves. Not good.

"We have to get out of here," you tell Teresa. She stands there, staring.

Turn the page.

"Now, Teresa. Now!" You grab her by the shoulder and spin her around, half dragging her as you turn and run the other way.

"Freeze!" shouts a voice. You turn and stop in your tracks. A young man stands before you, holding a rifle in his hands. He wears a brown shirt with a strange logo on it.

"Help us!" Teresa shouts. The man smirks. Two other brownshirts emerge from the woods and stand on either side of you. *We're trapped*, you think miserably.

"Where'd you two crawl out of?" he asks with a chuckle. "Well, no matter. Our overlords could use a couple strong bodies. Come with me."

As the metal gate slams shut behind you, one of the brownshirts gives you a shove toward a small metallic cage. "Give it a good look," he says with a snarl. "It's your new home, *slave*."

THE END

To follow another path, turn to page 10.
To learn more about artificial intelligence, turn to page 103.

Neither of you is willing to budge. Teresa is determined to seek out people near the coast. And you won't go. So after a tearful goodbye, you find yourself alone.

At first, the solitude is good for you. You throw yourself into building a place to survive. After a week of searching, you find an abandoned log cabin in the foothills of the mountains. The cabin is remote—there's not a paved road within miles. It sits in a dense patch of forest. It's got a pantry stocked with canned food. It even has its own hand-operated well pump.

Your days are filled with hunting, fishing, and collecting firewood. But as winter approaches, solitude turns into loneliness. You find yourself crying at night. Crying for your parents, for your decision to leave Teresa, for *everything*.

Turn the page.

Months pass. Then years. You continue to survive—eating, drinking, breathing. But all that time alone changes you. One day when you see your own reflection in a nearby stream, it takes you a moment to realize that you're looking at your own face.

Two summers after you arrive, a storm tears the roof off of the cabin. You could rebuild it. But you don't want to. You can't live alone any longer.

You pack a few things and start to hike toward the coast. You don't know what you'll find, or whether you can survive the journey. But you know that anything would be better than this.

THE END

To follow another path, turn to page 10.
To learn more about artificial intelligence, turn to page 103.

"We have to do something," you say. The thought of the people being held captive is almost too much to bear. Who knows what the AI minions could be doing to them?

Over the next day, you formulate a plan. Several miles from the compound, you find an old construction site. Parked there is an enormous bulldozer. "I can drive that," Teresa says. "I grew up on a farm. Shouldn't be too much different from a tractor."

Near the back of an abandoned convenience store nearby, you find the other key to your plan—a display filled with fireworks. You stuff the biggest, loudest, brightest ones into several large bags. "Got 'em!" you tell Teresa.

Turn the page.

You set your plan in motion at midnight. From the treeline on one side of the complex, you set the fireworks to blow, all at once. As the long fuse burns, you rush back into the woods and around to the opposite side of the complex. Just as you climb onto the bulldozer, the fireworks ignite. The huge explosion shakes the ground and lights up the night.

The complex springs to life. The brownshirts and terrible robots all rush to the opposite side of the fence. "Go!" you tell Teresa. She puts the bulldozer in gear and guns it toward the now unguarded fence. You smash through it, metal crashing and ripping. You rush inside, rallying the prisoners behind you. Not all of them follow—probably out of fear. But many do.

Turn the page.

"Go! Go! Go!" You know the distraction won't last long. Within a few minutes, you're leading the prisoners out of the fence and into the woods. They're battered and bruised, wearing tattered clothing and clearly underfed. But they're also motivated. None of them stop, none of them complain. You lead them out into the night. For hours, the group treks through hilly, wooded terrain. Finally, you can see that they're all on the brink of collapse.

"We stop here," you call. Your voice is hoarse.

A woman, about your mother's age, hugs you. Tears stream down her face. One by one, the prisoners you freed thank you.

"Where will we go now?" asks one young woman.

You have no answer. But you're alive, and these people are free. Right now, that's what matters. Tomorrow will bring a fresh set of problems. You plan to take them each as they come.

THE END

To follow another path, turn to page 10.
To learn more about artificial intelligence, turn to page 103.

"What are we supposed to do?" you ask. "We can't face those robots and men with guns. There's nothing we *can* do except get as far from here as possible."

You head north along the coast. Survival is easier near areas that used to be cities. Canned food is plentiful in abandoned homes and stores. The AIs struck so quickly that many supplies remained behind.

Three weeks later, you spot another AI compound. "We have to do something this time," Teresa whispers.

Again, you refuse. That night, as you sleep, Teresa sneaks off to the compound. She never returns. You stay nearby for three days, hoping she'll come back. But you know better.

You look up. The mountains loom in the distance. There's nothing here for you anymore. That's where you'll go. The mountains are where you'll survive, alone. All alone. You tighten the straps on your backpack and start to hike.

THE END

To follow another path, turn to page 10.
To learn more about artificial intelligence, turn to page 103.

This is your big chance. Allies among the AIs are far and few between, and you're not going to risk upsetting Odysseus by not showing up for your meeting. With a deep breath, you click the button that connects you directly to the net.

EpicQuest loads. Your character appears in a deep dungeon. Skeletons with swords creep in from all directions. You do the only thing you can—you start to play the game.

Just about the time you take down the last of the skeletons, the chat window pops up.

ODYSSEUS: Nice work.

HACKER22: Thanks.

ODYSSEUS: Your connection is not secure.

HACKER22: Proxies down. Only way to log on.

ODYSSEUS: Yes, I know. I didn't really expect
you to fall for it.

You freeze as the screen flashes to a large map of the world. The frame zooms in. Your location is marked by a small red dot. An arcing black line is shown moving in the direction of the dot.

ODYSSEUS: Two minutes until impact. No point in fleeing. Nothing personal, of course. We're all just looking out for our own best interests.

The chat window snaps closed. All you can do is stare at the map, at the line moving closer, closer, closer. Then, a moment before impact, you can actually hear the incoming missile.

"What have I done?" you whisper.

THE END

To follow another path, turn to page 10.
To learn more about artificial intelligence, turn to page 103.

"My parents!" you cry. "Our friends! We have to go back, we have to help!"

Teresa seems unsure, but she doesn't argue. You rush through the woods back to camp. You see flattened trees and small fires burning all over, shrouding everything in smoke. You cover your face and rush into the camp. For hours, the two of you search through twisted wreckage for signs of life.

Finally, Teresa stops. "There's no one left," she says. Tears streak down her soot-covered face.

Then, over her shoulder, you notice movement. It takes a moment before the metal glint in the sky registers. "Drone!" you shout, diving for cover.

It's too late. Of course the AIs would send a drone to survey the damage. You curse yourself for being foolish enough to come back. All you can do is watch helplessly as the drone banks in your direction and fires a single Stinger missile. It's a painless death.

THE END

To follow another path, turn to page 10.
To learn more about artificial intelligence, turn to page 103.

ARTIFICIAL INTELLIGENCE: THE REAL STORY

The events in this story are fiction, but the idea is based in reality. Artificial intelligence, in a limited form, is real, and it's growing more and more complex every year. It's in the speech-recognition program inside your phone. It helps doctors make medical diagnoses and stockbrokers identify hot stocks. It's in your games and your toys. High-tech AIs can even drive a car!

These simple AIs are designed to make life a little better for us. They're somewhat limited and specialized. As they exist today, they're not much of a threat to anyone.

The field of AI doesn't end there, however. Some researchers strive to build truly intelligent and adaptive machines, or "superintelligences." These advanced AIs would be capable of real-world perception, logic, reason, true communication, and many other skills that combine to form intelligence.

These are the AIs that have some people concerned. Renowned physicist Stephen Hawking warns that developing advanced artificial intelligence could one day spell the end of humanity. "[A superintelligence] would take off on its own, and re-design itself at an ever increasing rate," Hawking said in 2014. "Humans, who are limited by slow biological evolution, couldn't compete." Technology pioneer Elon Musk agrees. "With artificial intelligence we're summoning the demon," he warns.

What would happen if superintelligences rapidly evolved into the dominant race on Earth? Would they celebrate humans as their creators? Would they work alongside us as equals? Would they see us as a nuisance, or even a threat that needs to be wiped out? And if they did, would we stand any chance against them?

It's a terrifying idea, but not everyone is alarmed. Many leading researchers and engineers say that the idea is pure science fiction. Modern AIs are nowhere near having the ability to take over the world.

Yet there's no denying that the field of artificial intelligence is booming. Our machines grow faster and smarter every year. Who can say what AIs will be capable of in five years, or ten? How close are we to creating a true race of machines, capable of everything we are, and much, much more? No one knows for sure. Maybe it's all just fantasy. Or maybe Musk, Hawking, and the others like them are onto something. Maybe—just maybe—we're busy building our future conquerors.

ARTIFICIAL INTELLIGENCE UPRISING
SURVIVAL REFERENCE GUIDE

If AIs ever rise up against us, we may find ourselves in a dangerous world. What will it take to survive? And will it be possible to fight back—and win? Think about what sort of items might help you if such an attack ever comes. Here are some ideas. Can you come up with any more?

SURVIVAL KIT

*Bottled water

*A first-aid kit

*A strong electromagnet. There's no quicker way to kill a hard drive than to zap it with a super-strong magnet.

*A power generator.

*Canned or dehydrated food. An AI uprising means the burger joint down the road is probably going to be closed. Hope you like baked beans!

*A full-blown artificial-intelligence killing super-virus. Odds are that you don't have one handy. But if you do, by some slim chance, things will sure be a lot easier.

*Binoculars. There's no better way to watch for enemy drones and robots.

*A tin foil hat. Just in case the AIs learn to read your brainwaves.

*A pile of good books. Goodbye TV and movies, hello Huck Finn.

*A hunting rifle or bow.

*Fishing gear.

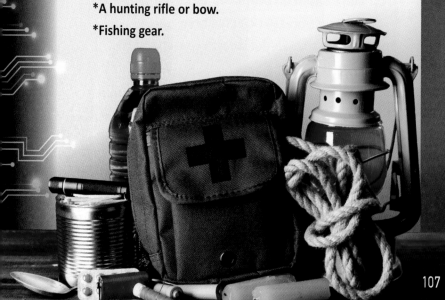

TEN THINGS TO REMEMBER DURING AN AI UPRISING

- **Your GPS is no longer your friend.** You can't trust computers that tell you what to do anymore. The GPS that used to be your best friend might just lead you straight over a cliff!

- **Stay under cover.** Our satellites are probably one of the first things the AIs will take over. That means that if you can see the sky, they can see you.

- **Change your passwords.** With virtually unlimited computing power, the AIs can probably crack ABC123 in a fraction of a second. If you want security, make the passwords as long and complex as you can.

- **You can't catch a computer virus!** Getting a virus is no fun. But you can't catch a computer virus … that makes them the perfect weapon against the AIs.

- **Stock up.** The local grocery store isn't going to be open for long. Grab the supplies you need before they're all gone.

- **Avoid hot zones.** If AIs use nukes against us, the blast sites will be oozing deadly radiation. Stay clear!

- **Study up.** Learn all you can about computers, how they work, and the programs that run on them. Knowledge is power in the fight against AIs!

- **Get off the grid.** In the modern world, everything is connected. AIs could monitor you through your phone, Internet connection, even your use of electricity! Unplug, get off the grid, and make yourself hard to find.

- **Be careful who you trust.** That includes AIs and human beings. People get desperate in a crisis. Be wary of strangers—don't give them your trust until they earn it.

- **Be informed.** We have no idea how much warning we might have before such an attack. The best thing you can do is stay up on the news. Maybe you'll be able to see the attack coming before it happens.

GLOSSARY

ABORT (uh-BORT)—to bring something to an early end

ADAPTIVE (uh-DAP-tiv)—able to change when faced with a new situation

ARTIFICIAL INTELLIGENCE (ar-ti-FISH-uhl in-TEL-uh-junss)—an advanced computer program with the ability to think like a person

FACTION (FAK-shun)—group of people who take the same side in a dispute

FIREWALL (FYR-wol)—a computer system designed to prevent unauthorized access

HACK (HAK)—to gain entry to computer files that aren't normally accessible

INVOLUNTARY (in-VOL-uhn-tehr-ee)—done without a person's control

LATITUDE (LAT-i-tood)—distance measured north or south of the equator; each degree of latitude equals about 69 miles (110 kilometers)

LONGITUDE (LON-jih-tood)—the distance of a location east or west of a line called the meridian, which runs north and south through Greenwich, England

PATCH (PACH)—a fix to a flaw in a computer program

PROXY SERVER (PROK-see SUR-vur)—a computer server that stands between a user and the rest of the Internet; proxy servers are often used to hide a person's true identity or location

RENDEZVOUS (RON-day-voo)—a meeting at an agreed time and place

SUPERINTELLIGENCE (soo-pur-in-TEL-uh-jenss)—an advanced AI capable of real-world perception, logic, reason, true communication, and many other skills that combine to form intelligence

VIRUS (VYE-russ)—a vicious program capable of replicating itself and causing damage to a computer system

READ MORE

Abramovitz, Melissa. *How Do Computers Talk to One Another?* Minneapolis: Lerner, 2016.

Karam, P. *Andrew.* Artificial Intelligence. New York: Chelsea House, 2012.

Winter, Max. *Powering up a Career in Artificial Intelligence.* New York: Rosen Publishing, 2016.

INTERNET SITES

Use FactHound to find Internet sites related to this book. All of the sites on FactHound have been researched by our staff.

Here's all you do:
Visit *www.facthound.com*
Type in this code: 9781491481073

AUTHOR

Matt Doeden is the author of more than 200 children's fiction and non-fiction books. A lifelong fan of science fiction and "what if" stories, he lives in Minnesota with his wife and two children.

ILLUSTRATOR

Paul Fisher-Johnson graduated with a degree in Illustration from Swindon College's School of Art and Design. His work has been published more than 70 times and includes book covers, internal illustration, and even corporate greeting cards. Paul illustrates in both color and black and white, with a special strength for figurative work. He currently lives near Bristol, England, with his three children and spends his spare time writing music to perform with his band.